IMAGES OF ENGLAND

NEWCASTLE-
UNDER–LYME
SCHOOL

IMAGES OF ENGLAND

NEWCASTLE-
UNDER–LYME
SCHOOL

CAROLINE DAVIS

TEMPUS

Frontispiece: An aerial view of Newcastle-under-Lyme School in 1985. While the extent of buildings make the expansion of the school clear, it excludes the AstroTurf, Sports Hall, Sixth Form Centre, Memorial Hall extension and Pre-Preparatory and Nursery Department which were all added in the following twenty years.

First published 2005

Tempus Publishing Limited
The Mill, Brimscombe Port,
Stroud, Gloucestershire, GL5 2QG
www.tempus-publishing.com

British Library Cataloguing in Publication Data.
A catalogue record for this book is available from the British Library.

ISBN 0 7524 3631 4

Typesetting and origination by Tempus Publishing Limited.
Printed in Great Britain.

Contents

Acknowledgements

I am indebted to a large number of people who have contributed their time, memories and photographs to support the development of this book. In particular, Gabrielle Beard and Cynthia Smart have provided invaluable support – including Latin translation services! Now in their nineties, Jake Barton and Ruth Bennett have exceptionally long associations with the schools, and each has a remarkably strong memory which has enabled many facts to be established and faces to be identified. In addition, a large number of pupils and staff, both past and present, have also been a source of expertise about specific eras and willing points of reference. With apologies to anyone I have inadvertently omitted, these include Dorothy Bathurst, Pat Bishop, Claire Bloor, Rosemary Bowcock, Mary Bowdler, Reg Brooks, Dave Buckingham, Wendy Butler, Ian Cartwright, Rosemary Chawner, Gordon Collis, Enid Dawson, Rob Dillow, Bill Donaldson, Jean Fletcher, Graham Forrester, Ann Foster, Elaine Garrett, Angela Hartill, Norah Hill, Christopher Johnson, Michêle Laine, Maureen Leese, Susan Lodge, Lesley Ollerenshaw, Kath Miller, Rosemary Morrey, Jean Nicholas, John Nicholas, Gillian Norbury, Gail Parker, Frank Priddle, Ken Rhead, Dave Sawyer, Peter Scragg, Alan Sherratt, Frederick Smith, Joy Sugden, Paul Thomas, Helen Tucker, John Wain, Erica Watson, Susan Webb, Betty Williams, Michael Wood and Ann Wotherspoon.

I also acknowledge with thanks permission to use photographs provided by *The Sentinel*, Louisa Warham, Ernest Warrilow (who also took many of the *Sentinel* photographs), Paula Hannant and Aerofilms.

As always, love and appreciation to my husband Tim and my children Jack and Harry for their patience over the last year.

In 1929, Kathleen Griffiths (Upper IV C) embroidered this Orme Girls' shield and presented it to the school. It was initially hung in the headmistress's room, but can now be seen in the Victoria Library, alongside a copy that was made in class by about sixty girls.

Introduction

'I always find it difficult to give you even a glimpse of the many and varied activities which go on outside the classroom throughout the year – and this is not through paucity of material but, on the contrary, because of its overwhelming abundance.' While Sheila Smith, Orme Girls' headmistress, faced this difficulty in deciding what to include in her 1965 Prize Giving address, the scale of the dilemma was far greater when selecting from the abundance of material available for inclusion in this pictorial glimpse into the past of Newcastle-under-Lyme School (NULS) and both its predecessors, Newcastle High and Orme Girls' Schools. The challenge has been deciding what to omit rather than what to include.

In recent years, the school's archive material from the 1870s to the present day has been collated. This includes factual records, such as registers of admissions and leavers, logbooks, Prize Giving speeches and programmes, school society minute books and the magazines produced by both the schools and the former pupil societies. More importantly for developing this book for the *Images of England* series, the archives include a large number of photographs which bring to life the historical records and offer their own record of school buildings, school life and customs, notable occasions and, most vividly, some of the many individuals associated with the schools. The school archives have also been enlivened by individual contributions which incorporate personal stories and experiences. Hopefully the published material captures the range of what is available and will arouse interest, perhaps amusement and, in some cases, nostalgia.

The recording of material about the High School was started by its first headmaster, Francis Kitchener. He produced what he described as a School Register, in which he recorded the names of all school Governors, staff and pupils – including their dates of attendance and addresses – and, from 1880, a school magazine, *The Fire-Fly*, that regularly recorded school events and achievements. In 1893, Kitchener suggested this was 'somewhat laborious, although very interesting', but he was confident it would be of great value to future historians. How right he was!

When collating the archives, efforts have been made to put names to faces, and one example illustrates how the information compiled by Kitchener has been used within this book. While the names of Kitchener's staff are recorded, and the archives include a picture of them, only two names can be put to the faces – Kitchener and Henry Phillips, who taught French and German. Phillips was identified through a combination of Kitchener's register of Masters and subjects taught, the *Fire-Fly* which mentions the Natural History Society (of which Phillips was a member) visiting Swynnerton in 1899, a photograph labelled simply 'Group Swynnerton', and early photographs of an unnamed French and German teacher, who is recognisable on the Swynnerton photograph. Henry Phillips' obituary in the 1938 *Fire-Fly* recalls 'his close-cropped beard comparing favourably with the somewhat more Victorian hirsute adornments of the headmaster and other members of the staff' – identity confirmed!

While no guarantee can be offered regarding the factual accuracy of this book, a great deal of effort has been put into trying to avoid errors. The identity of Phillips is one example, but all of the dates and names indicated have been cross-referenced against contemporary sources rather than relying on what might be expected to be impeccable information. For example, staff member Miss Nance wrote in the *Orme Girls' School Magazine* about her own time as a pupil at the school. Interestingly the Leavers Register indicated that Miss Nance was a pupil in (slightly) different years, and the dates recorded in this book are from the Register rather than her own recollection.

While the High School and Orme Girls' were separate institutions until 1981, there have always been links between the two. In particular, the schools had shared Governors – the Governors of the Newcastle Endowed Schools. Thanks to educational endowments that can be traced to the beginning of the seventeenth century, the Governors were able, in 1873, to let a contract for the provision of two sets of school buildings. This contract, written in copperplate handwriting, listing the Governors' names and their widely differing occupations, was followed a year later by a letter from the builders presenting an increased estimate for the work 'caused by the advance in prices of labour and the scarcity of same'. Nonetheless, Newcastle High School for Boys duly opened in 1874 and Orme Girls', the first secondary school for girls in North Staffordshire, in 1876.

As a High School motto, Kitchener chose *Nunquam non Nova*, 'not new things but in a new way'. The Orme Girls' motto was *Summa Sequendo*, 'by aiming for the highest'. With a history full of change and continual development whilst aiming at the same time for the highest possible standards, the schools have lived up to these mottos. Both schools were fee-paying until, following the 1944 Education Act, they assumed Voluntary Aided Status in 1949. Fee-paying returned in September 1981 when educational policy changes led to the two schools combining as one independent school – Newcastle-under-Lyme School – although boys and girls continued to be taught separately. A mixed Preparatory Department, Orme House, opened in 1982. As long ago as 1913, an Orme Girls' inspection report commented on the potential impact 'of widening the scope of the school by opening a Kindergarten Department'. This vision was finally realised when a Pre-Preparatory and Nursery Department was added to the school in 2004, occupying a purpose-built extension to Orme House. In carefully planned stages, the whole school is also becoming co-educational, with 2004 being the last year in which the Senior School had single sex intakes.

Its earlier pupils would no doubt find it hard to recognise a picture of the school as it stands today. Yet the documents, photographs and personal memories which present the school's earlier history reveal at every stage untiring efforts on the part of Governors, headmasters, headmistresses and many other individuals, to establish and maintain the high standards which have provided such a firm foundation for the present Newcastle-under-Lyme School.

Newcastle High School headmasters

Francis Kitchener	1873 to 1891
George Rundall	1891 to 1900
Fred Harrison	1901 to 1925
Tom Stinton	1926 to 1948
Jim Todd	1948 to 1963
John Roberts	1964 to 1972
Bill Donaldson	1974 to 1981

Orme Girls' headmistresses

Mary Martin	1876 to 1891
Margaret Powell	1891 to 1919
Jessie Sprunt	1919 to 1938
Noël Paterson	1938 to 1939
Elnith Kemp	1940 to 1951
Sheila Smith	1952 to 1968
Freda Buxton	1969 to 1980
Hilary Ludlum	1980 to 1981

Newcastle-under-Lyme School principals

Bill Donaldson	1982 to 1990
Ray Reynolds	1990 to 2002
Rob Dillow	2002

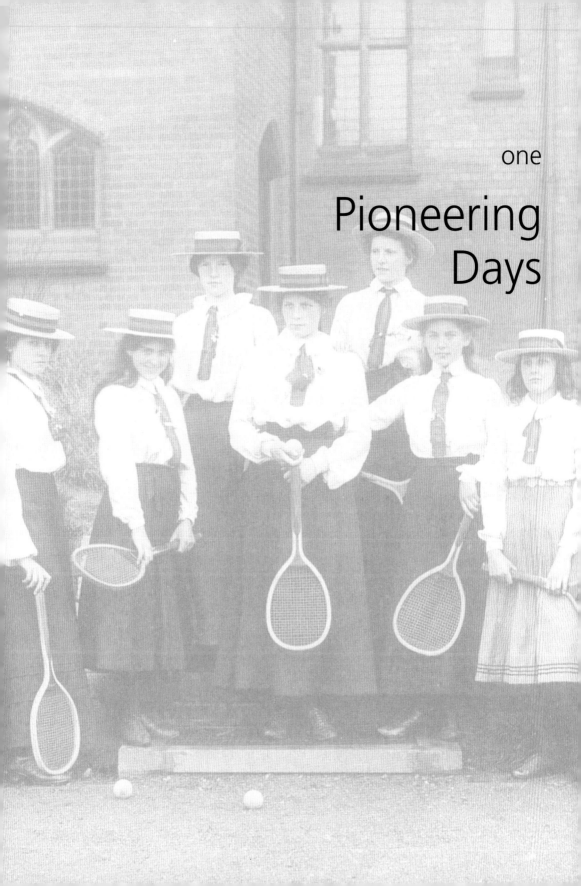

one

Pioneering
Days

In the middle of the nineteenth century, separate endowed schools were educating boys in Newcastle-under-Lyme. The Endowed Schools Act, 1869, provided an opportunity to consolidate the various endowments and reconsider the educational needs of the borough. Under the guidance of the first Chairman of Governors of the Newcastle Endowed Schools, Mr W.H. Dutton, this prompted the establishment of a new 'First Grade School', Newcastle High School, in 1874 and, as 'simply an experiment', the Orme Girls' School in 1876.

Pictured here with his mother is Dr Frederick Temple, Rugby School headmaster and later Archbishop of Canterbury, who laid the High School foundation stone in September 1874. Dutton's son attended Rugby School and he contacted Temple about the establishment of the High School. Temple recommended Francis Kitchener, his Assistant Master, as headmaster. Kitchener subsequently wrote Temple's memoirs, published in 1907.

While the new High School was being built, between April 1874 to April 1876, classes were held in the Congregational Chapel, which is still in King Street. J.W. Harding was the first boy entered at the temporary school – he died aged twenty-three as a result of drowning while bathing in Lake Killarney. When the boys vacated the Congregational Rooms, the Orme Girls' moved in for a year.

Above: Sixty-nine applications were received when Kitchener was appointed as the first High School headmaster. Taken in what is now the Lancaster site staff car park, this is the only known photograph of Kitchener and his staff. Kitchener was first cousin of Lord Kitchener, the renowned Secretary for War. Seated, second left, is Henry Phillips and, fourth left, Kitchener, who recorded that, out of his first staff, nine went on to become headmasters and two professors. The school now owns Kitchener's gown.

Right: Appointed at the age of thirty-four, Miss Martin was Orme Girls' headmistress from 1876 to 1891. In its opening year, the school had fifty-four girls and a staff of four, including Miss Martin. She lived at 1 Lancaster Road and wore black throughout her headship. Even when talking among themselves, Miss Martin did not permit the girls to use Christian names, a rule which also applied to herself and her staff.

Left: An advertisement for both schools appeared in the *Staffordshire Times* in 1878. Public instruction in Practical Chemistry was also offered on Friday evenings – an early example of the High School running evening classes. Dr F. Clowes taught at the High School from 1876 to 1881 before leaving to become Professor of Chemistry at University College, Nottingham and later Chief Chemist to the London County Council.

Below: Having previously been Assistant Master at Rugby School, Kitchener is credited with introducing rugby to the Newcastle area. This picture of the 1881-82 First XV is now reproduced in the Dutton Dining Room. The captain (holding the ball) was George St John Topham. Two further players, Archibald Patten and Ernest Lever, were boarders whose photographs appear in the book presented to Kitchener when he left in 1891.

When he left in July 1891, Kitchener was presented with an album of photographs of past and present boys who had boarded with him. This boarder, Harry Johnson, joined the family business, Johnson Brothers of Hanley, before starting H. & R. Johnson Ltd and building it up to become one of the most important tile factories in North Staffordshire. He was taken prisoner in France during the First World War and awarded the DSO.

Ernest Lever attended the High School from 1879 to 1882. He was one of the fifty-eight founder members of the Old Newcastilians (ONs) in Summer 1892 and a member of the committee. He was President of the ONs in 1909. The Cambridge University ON Club, started in 1887, was Lever's idea.

Margaret Powell was an enlightened headmistress, educating the girls as citizens as well as academics. She introduced the use of pupils' Christian names; local trips, such as picnics at Moreton Hall; visits to the Lake District and Wales; and hockey, cricket and netball. She retired in 1919, aged seventy-one. In 1931, the Old Girls provided a memorial tablet in the Victoria Library and endowed a prize in her memory.

Entitled 'The Headmaster Responds', this photograph shows the boys being addressed in Big School (now the Memorial Hall) on Speech Day, *c.* 1892. Speaker George William Rundall was headmaster from 1891 to 1900. He had previously taught at Marlborough College. From 1902 to 1908 he was Registrar to the Teachers' Registration Council.

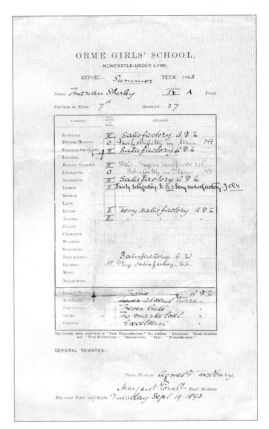

Right: Agnes Westbury, one of the Orme Girls' first pupils, signed Marian Shirley's 1893 school report. Agnes, daughter of the Vicar of Hartshill, taught Scripture at the school for forty-three years, the longest-serving Orme Girls' staff member. For many years, Agnes' parents ran the Boarding House on Marsh Parade.

Below: Kitchener used this picture of the school in the *High School Register, 1874 to 1894.* This recorded the history of the school and its endowments, plus the names of all school Governors, staff and pupils – including their dates of attendance and addresses. A cherry tree to match that shown in the foreground was planted as part of the 1974 centenary celebrations.

The first known school photograph was taken in 1895, with Headmaster G.W. Rundall in the centre. Robert Ferguson, author of *The Short Life of T.E. Hulme*, had the negative enlarged to identify Hulme, aged twelve (standing, ninth from left). Renowned as a poet and philosopher, Hulme was killed in Flanders in 1917, aged thirty-four. T.S. Elliot called him 'the forerunner of the twentieth-century mind'.

This plaque, now in the Dutton Dining Room, translates: 'To the Glory of God, the Best and Greatest, and in memory of W.H. Dutton, who, as Chairman of the Board of Governors, had looked after the interests of this school for twenty-six years with the greatest devotion, this tile has been dedicated by both those who are at present pupils and those who were pupils in the past, and now belong to the association of Newcastilians 1896'.

Henry Phillips (seated, centre) studied at Rugby School and Cambridge University. He joined the High School as French and German Master in 1875, aged twenty-five, and retired in 1910 with a £35 annual allowance. Entitled 'How We Learn German', the picture is from an album compiled by the school Photographic Society, of which Phillips was a member.

A horse-drawn roller on the Lower Close around 1898, where the school air-raid shelters were in 1939 and the AstroTurf can now be found. To make use of this area, the Close Improvement Fund was established to pay for levelling and other improvements. The High School was relatively compact at the turn of the century, with the buildings in the background being the full extent of the school.

At the turn of the century, Henry Phillips photographed R. Hornby (with Lancaster Road in the background). An Oxford graduate, Hornby was Senior Science Master at the High School, teaching there from 1894 to 1901. He sang *The Skipper* in the school's 1898 concert, in which Mr Rundall's wife played the contra-bass. In 1902, Hornby donated two guineas to the Dutton Building Fund.

The Natural History Society organised a range of outings that often included visiting historic buildings. The outings included Astbury Church, Swynnerton, Cheddleton, Moreton Old Hall and Mow Cop. A number of photographs of the outings survive, including this June 1899 trip to Swynnerton.

An Oxford graduate, Fred Harrison (centre) was headmaster from January 1901 to December 1925. Paid an annual salary of £200 plus residence, he became headmaster at the age of thirty-five. Under his leadership, Founders' Day and the Dutton Wing laboratories were established, and 'Big School' was transformed into the Memorial Hall.

Kitchener in 1904. An ardent promoter of education in Staffordshire, he had a record of educational dedication. For example, while at Rugby it was decided Botany should be taught. Kitchener studied Botany for five months before teaching it, including studying under the Great Curator at Kew Gardens and working in Barmouth with Professor Henslow for seven weeks. While at Newcastle, Kitchener taught Botany at both the High School and Orme Girls'.

Beatrice Yates (second from right) was captain of the 1904 tennis team and is named on the Honours Board opposite the Victoria Library entrance. Miss Powell rarely missed watching home tennis matches. The school has a book of wild flowers and leaves that Beatrice collected and pressed during the 1904 summer holidays.

A 1905 Board of Education Inspection Report described Miss Powell as 'very well qualified for her post, a good scholar and a good teacher, a woman of breadth and vigour. The school … is well organised and efficient.' An example of Miss Powell's approach was 'At Home' day – an open invitation to former and present pupils, parents and friends. An Old Girls' tennis match was usually included. This 1904 'At Home' day was before the 1908 Assembly Hall (the present Victoria Library) and other extensions were built.

Miss Grimes, VB Form Mistress in 1904, had to leave the school because she married. She subsequently died in childbirth. While at the Orme, she started the fiction library in 1906 – subscription 6d per term. During the return from one of Miss Powell's picnics at Hanchurch Wood, the girls wanted to give three cheers for Miss Grimes – but she asked them not to for fear of frightening the horses.

Hockey was introduced at the High School in 1894 and, until 1922, the girls played on the High School pitches. The 1905 hockey team wore navy blue skirts with three rows of red braid round the hem. They are looking towards where the Sydney Myott Wing was to be built in 1963. Mabel Whitfield (standing, second from right) was Sydney Myott's sister-in-law.

Part of the 'Newcastle' series of postcards, this 1907 watercolour shows the front of the Orme Girls' School. The first school building cost £2,000. There was no road access to the site; Victoria Road was constructed as part of the scheme.

Named in honour of the first Chairman of Governors, the Dutton Wing provided new science laboratories. Eminent scientist Sir Oliver Lodge, whose son attended the High School, opened it in 1903. Provision was made in the design for 'the carrying out of the modern idea that boys should learn to see and think for themselves'. Hanslip Fletcher sketched the Chemistry laboratory in 1913. This became the Dutton Dining Room in 1991.

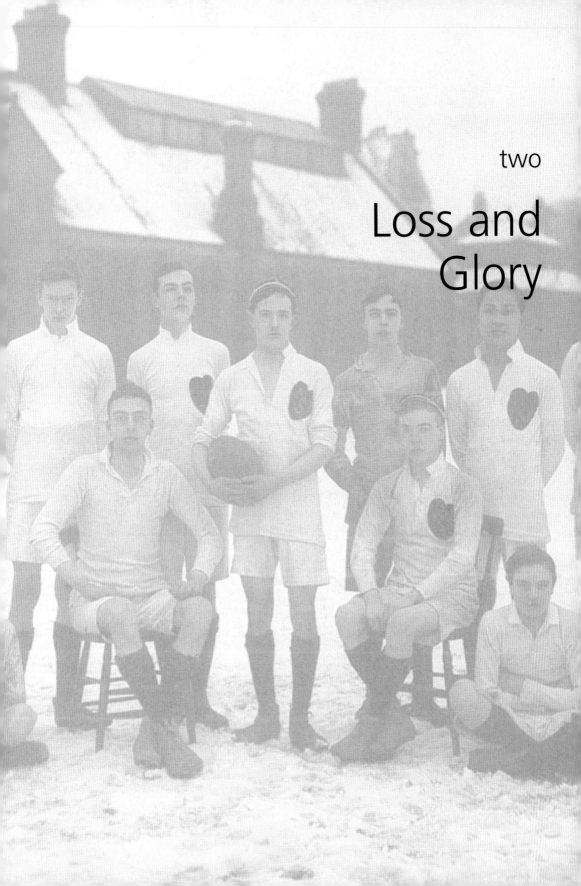

two

Loss and Glory

The 5 September 1914 *Sentinel* front page included the headline 'Old Boys for the New Army' and reported that 'Boys from Newcastle High School responded cheerfully to the call to war and marched to Stoke Station'. In common with the country in general, the impact of the First World War on the schools was substantial. Ninety-one ONs were killed in action. Six DSOs were awarded, thirty-five Military Crosses, one Distinguished Service Cross, one Distinguished Flying Cross and one Military Medal. The Orme Girls' also supported the war effort, serving in military hospitals, fundraising, inviting wounded soldiers in the local hospital to tea, supporting two prisoners of war in Germany and undertaking traditionally male jobs.

Above: Mr Loodden, pictured with his mechanics, gave exhibition flights from the school football field from 1-4 July 1914.

Left: Head of School Reginald Mellor putting the weight in 1914. In a 1911 High School debate, Mellor spoke in favour of the motion that 'Arbitration is preferable to war'. During the First World War, he was to be awarded the Military Cross for rescuing wounded soldiers in his battery. He went on to study a shortened post-war course at Sidney Sussex, Cambridge.

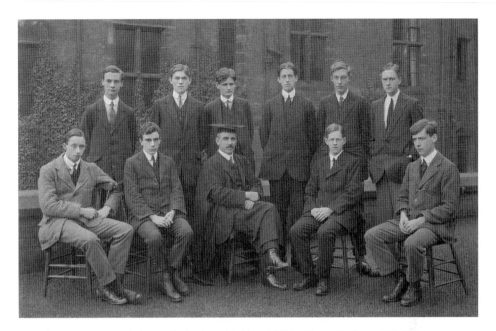

Praepostors, 1914. From left to right, back row: Adams, Philbin, Hurst, Hosband, Hill, Salt (see page 93). Front row: Mellor, Stevenson, Mr Harrison, Leese, Powell. Both Adams and Hill received the Military Cross, as did Mellor and thirty-two others from the school. Stevenson was awarded the DFC.

In 1915, the boarders included two Siamese pupils who had previously been educated at a Government School in Siam. The Siamese Legation sent them to Newcastle, with their guardian's address being in London. Huat won School Colours for playing in the Rugby XV (third from right, back row). A 1916 report from the match with Willaston School records that Huat scored a try, but the conversion was unsuccessful.

With the approval of the Army Council, a company of the Officer Training Corps (OTC) had been formed at the School in 1908. As part of the war effort, boys from the High School attended the OTC wood-cutting camp at Hodnet during the Easter 1917 holiday, being billeted in the stables at Hodnet Hall. The boys felled trees and helped in the timberyard.

Master Jackie Barton (standing, centre) with the High School Cricket XI, 1918. Captain G.A.F. Bagguley (seated, centre) was President of the ON Club when the Memorial Cricket Pavilion was opened in 1955. Barton taught at the High School for thirty-six years and was closely associated with the Cricket XI. Cricket was first played at the High School in 1877. In an 1884 match against Trentham, Master Mr Cooper scored the school's first century.

Members of the Cambridge ON Club in Easter Term 1919. From left to right, back row: Farrall, Nation, Hay, Parr. Front row: G. Pickering, Salt (see page 93), Harrison, Green, Mellor, R.C. Pickering. Four other members were absent. The club was started in 1887 and restarted in 1919 following the war. *The Fire-Fly* included regular letters detailing life at Cambridge, starting with the first issue in 1880.

Miss Dorothy Stedman (centre) with members of Remove A on a 1919 Botany Picnic. In Kitchener's time, a number of the girls were taught Science by High School Masters. Kitchener's wife, Frances Anna Hammond, gave Botany lectures to Orme Girls' pupils and staff, and wrote a textbook, *A Year's Botany for Schools*. After his death, a collection of Kitchener's works, mostly on Botany, were donated to the Orme Girls'.

Seventy-eight applications were received when thirty-three-year-old Miss Jessie Sprunt, with a first-class honours degree in Modern Languages, was appointed Orme Girls' headmistress in 1919. Among other initiatives before she left in 1938, Miss Sprunt encouraged the girls to take part in Games – only 50% played games regularly in 1924. By 1930, none asked for exemption except on the grounds of health.

In 1919, Christmas plays resumed. The High School boys and Masters performed scenes from Shakespeare's *Twelfth Night* and *A Midsummer Night's Dream*, and Moliere's *Les Precieuses Ridicules*. While hailing the success of the evening, *The Fire-Fly* also records that McKenzie 'should remember that a Shakespearean countess seldom takes a yard stride'.

Above: Ida Blaney (left) with Winifred Wainwright. Ida subsequently married Dunbar Bishop, who chaired the Swimming Baths Appeal. Winifred was captain of the First XI cricket, and Ida was the wicketkeeper. Miss Balsillie, who took the photograph, was Drill and Games Mistress from January 1919 to July 1920.

Right: Records were kept of the physical measurements of pupils, such as these recorded for Donald Watkin in 1920. In addition to his termly measurements, Donald's academic reports, 'honourable mentions', school blazer and Old Boys' tie have been donated to the school. Donald was a pupil at the High School from 1917 to 1923.

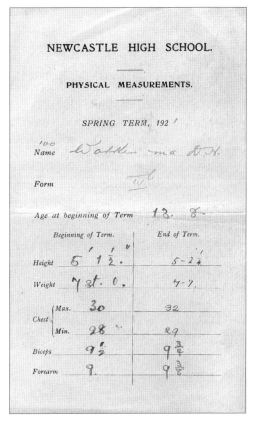

NEWCASTLE HIGH SCHOOL.

PHYSICAL MEASUREMENTS.

SPRING TERM, 192 /

Name *Watki ma D.H.*

Form

Age at beginning of Term   13. 8.

	Beginning of Term.	End of Term.
Height	5′ 1½″	5 - 2¼′
Weight	7 st. 0.	7 - 7.
Chest { Max.	30	32
Chest { Min.	28	29
Biceps	9½	9¾
Forearm	9.	9⅜

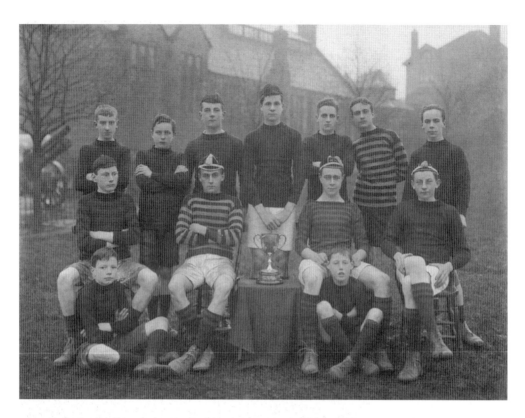

Mr C. Grant Robinson talking to Miss Sprunt in 1921. Robinson was Principal of the University of Birmingham when he addressed the 1921 High School Founders' Day and Prize Distribution and the 1923 Orme Girls' annual Prize Giving, held in the Municipal Hall.

Parents and friends leaving the hall after the High School Prize Distribution in 1921. David Barritt, later Chairman of Governors, won the Miles Settle Prize. He attended the High School from 1917 to 1922, was Head of School and Captain of the Football XI.

Opposite above: The West House XV, 1920. To foster intra-school competition, in 1903 the boys were divided into houses depending on where they lived – North (Hanley, Burslem, Basford, Leek), School (boarders and Stoke) and West (elsewhere). A portion of those who lived in Newcastle were allocated to each house. East House was added in 1926.

Opposite below: Second XI hockey, 1921-22. From left to right, standing: M. Barlow, W. Barratt, E. Heath, C. Duddell, C. Woolley, A. Billington, B. Stewart. Seated: A. Wright, A. Talbot, K. Mellor, J. Hancock, P. Goldstraw. A plaque in the Victoria Library records Winifred Barratt's benefactions, which include the £50,000 bequest that funded the purchase of houses in Vessey Terrace that now constitute the Art, Music and Home Economics Departments (the Barratt Centre). When the School House System changed in 1991, one house was also named after her.

In March 1922, the Upper and Lower VI girls performed Moliere's *Les Femmes Savantes*. Language teacher Miss Peel (third left) introduced each act, explaining the plot to the audience of friends and parents.

Orme Girls' School, Newcastle-under-Lyme

October 1922.

Latin teacher Miss H.M. Barnard (fifth staff member from the left) wrote the Orme Girls' song *Floreamus* during the 1926-27 school year. The tune was that used at Stamford School, where her father was headmaster. Second from the left among the staff is Miss Westbury, who signed the 1893 report reproduced earlier.

Right: Having raised £4,000 through a public appeal, 'Big School' was transformed into the Memorial Hall. A tablet was unveiled on Founders' Day 1923. Prior to his main address, Colonel Campbell VC, who commanded a North Staffordshire Brigade during the war, said: 'We unveil this tablet in memory of our brothers who laid down their lives in the war'. The tablet was then dedicated by the Bishop of Stepney, an ON.

Below: Of the boys who had passed through the High School since it first opened, about one third served in the forces and, of those, one in five had lost their lives. The Memorial Hall scheme involved oak panelling up to the corbels and erecting an organ gallery. Completion of the work coincided with the High School Jubilee, 1924. The organ was officially inaugurated in November when the Liverpool Cathedral organist gave a recital.

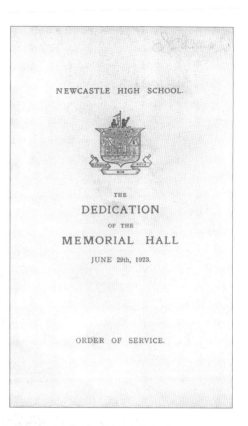

NEWCASTLE HIGH SCHOOL.

THE

DEDICATION

OF THE

MEMORIAL HALL

JUNE 29th, 1923.

ORDER OF SERVICE.

THE HIGH SCHOOL NEWCASTLE STAFFS - MEMORIAL HALL.

An unusual view of the Orme Girls' School before the gymnasium was built on the tennis court.

Founders' Day was first marked by the Orme Girls' in 1921. A memorial plaque to founder Edward
Orme can be found in St Giles' Church, where he is buried in the churchyard. The first girls' Founders'
Day service to be held at St Giles was in 1936. In 1924, the principal speaker on Founders' Day was
Prebendary C. Dunkley (seated, left), Chairman of the Staffordshire Education Committee.

For a number of years, Sir Reginald Hardy, a Governor, invited some of the Orme Girls to his home near Tutbury, Dunstall Hall. Twelve girls attended the 1924 visit. They spent the day looking at art treasures and rambling in the gardens. English teacher Miss Welland, who taught at the school from 1917 to 1950 and continued part time until 1955, accompanied the girls.

His Majesty King George V chatting with the Mayor of Newcastle and Fred Harrison, headmaster of Newcastle High School, prior to inspecting the school's Officer Training Corp in 1925.

The 1925 Science VI with Form Master Gilbert 'Gus' Clough. Gus taught at the High School from 1919 to 1953, as Senior Science Master from 1921, and was House Master of West House. He played a key role in supporting school life after the First World War, taking part in many sports, leading the hockey team and fostering the Arts and Sciences Society. In 1987, his son, Francis, married Hilary Ludlam, the last Orme Girls' headmistress.

A hatless Miss Sprunt with her staff in 1926. St Paul's Schoolrooms, seen in the background, provided accomodation for the expanding girls' school.

The Orme Girls' in its Jubilee year, 1926. When the school was opened in 1876, it was believed that it would accommodate 100 pupils and that this would be quite sufficient. Time soon proved this wrong, with continual overcrowding problems encountered. Over 350 pupils attended the school by 1926.

Above left: Louisa Warham at her father's photographic studio in Audley. Louisa attended the school from 1926 to 1933 and took a number of photographs of school life. In common with many girls, she travelled to school by train – using Bignall End and Newcastle stations. A 1924 Inspection Report suggested that the reliance on trains was problematic because of late arrivals and the need to leave early to catch return trains.

Above right: In 1928 Katie Hitchings (standing, far right) became the first Orme Girls' pupil to study Law at Oxford. Emily Barber (standing, far left) is breaching the uniform regulations by wearing her maroon girdle too low! In 1932 the regulation girdle was altered to be maroon and blue, which Miss Sprunt recorded was because other schools were adopting similarly coloured girdles.

The weather was glorious for the 1929 High School Athletic Sports. Phillips won the obstacle race. Prizes were distributed in the Memorial Hall by Mrs Stinton, after which tea was provided in the Physics laboratory.

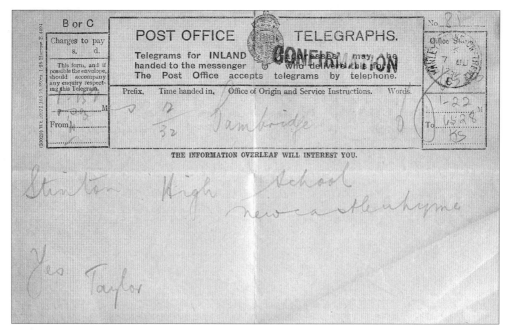

John Henry Taylor's 1929 telegram accepting an offer of appointment as Biology Master. Taylor was central to the expansion of Biology teaching in the High School. He was responsible for entrance examinations and the timetable; was Master in charge of cricket and playing fields; coached junior rugby for sixteen years; and was Second Master from 1952 until retiring in 1970.

three

Continued
Expansion

Both schools benefited from substantial extensions at the start of the 1930s, allowing increased numbers to be accommodated. Sir Henry Hadow CBE, Lord Lieutenant of the County and Chairman of the Consultative Committee of the Board of Education, which produced the Hadow Report on Education of the Adolescent, officially opened the new buildings on both sites in 1930.

An opening ceremony at the Municipal Hall followed Hadow's tour of inspection of the new buildings at both schools. Speakers included the Bishop of Lichfield, Sir William Goodwin (Chairman of Governors), the Earl of Harrowby (centre, right), Sir Henry Hadow (centre), Mr Whitehouse (Chairman of the Staffordshire Education Committee), Mr Weston Poole (Vice-Chairman of Governors), Miss Sprunt and Mr Stinton.

The new £16,550 High School building on the Upper Close, opposite the Memorial Hall, consisted of new classrooms, a gymnasium, Art room, music room, Masters' common room and laboratory. The New Buildings, now B Block, were often cold because of the open walkways on each floor. The gymnasium is now the Lancaster site library.

The Orme Girls' extensions cost £13,183 and consisted of a gymnasium, laboratory, new classrooms and a covered way linking the main and new building. Courtesy of a friendly bricklayer, the wall of the covered way includes an envelope containing the names of two Orme Girls' pupils, Janet Peasegood and Dorothy Makinson, which was cemented into the structure between two stones when it was built in 1930.

At the request of Gym Mistress Miss Barlow, Louisa Warham photographed the Orme Girls' gymnasium in 1931. Louisa recalls how Miss Barlow was enthused by the new facility. Miss Sprunt reported at Prize Giving in 1934 on progress made in gymnastic work since the provision of the gymnasium in 1930, culminating in two very successful displays given in the Municipal Hall in January that year.

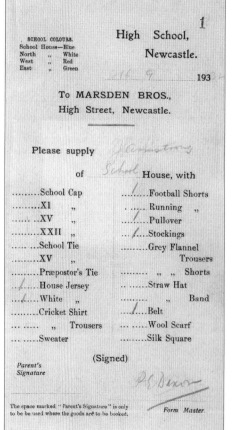

High School,
Newcastle.

1

............193

To MARSDEN BROS.,
High Street, Newcastle.

Please supply

of .... House, with

........School Cap
........XI „
........XV „
........XXII „
........School Tie
........XV „
........Præpostor's Tie
........House Jersey
........White „
........Cricket Shirt
.... „ Trousers
........Sweater

........Football Shorts
........Running „
........Pullover
........Stockings
........Grey Flannel
........Trousers
.... „ „ Shorts
........Straw Hat
.... „ Band
........Belt
........Wool Scarf
........Silk Square

(Signed)

Parent's
Signature

The space marked " Parent's Signature " is only
to be be used where the goods are to be booked.

Form Master.

Above: The Victoria Library in 1931, following the conversion of the Assembly Hall. The Honours Board (top left) was designed by Gordon Forsyth, Principal of the Burslem School of Art, to record First Class Honours and scholarships. In 1958, to accommodate the large number of academic successes, a second board was added above the door on the right.

Left: Armstrong lived in Liverpool Road, Newcastle in 1932 and was in School House. His uniform list was signed by P.E. Dixon who, in addition to undertaking clerical work, taught Mathematics and Science at the High School from 1923 to 1949. Dixon died within two months of leaving the school.

Opposite above: Headmaster Tom Stinton (centre right) outside the headmaster's house with 1932 boarders and staff. Boarding on site stopped in 1937. The window on the right was the lounge, now the principal's office. To the left, the present reception area, was the dining room with domestic headquarters below.

Opposite below: During Easter 1933, the Orme Girls' hosted a ten-day International School as a means of fostering understanding among young people from different countries. Twelve French and twelve German girls attended. In addition to discussion groups, trips to Chester and Dovedale were included, and the girls performed the play *Amicitia*.

Above: Miss Nance at the wheel of her car during the International School, with Miss Sprunt in the rear. Car ownership was rare at the time. Miss Nance was a pupil at the school from 1890 to 1897, and a member of staff from 1912 to 1943. In 1931, Arnold & Co. published her *A Text-Book of Needlework* that covered the School Certificate Examination syllabus. The cover was made in an unfadable and moisture-proof cloth.

Left: In May 1934 the Orme Girls' staff performed J.M. Barrie's *Quality Street*. The proceeds from this and school choir concerts enabled the stage to be raised and the library to be catalogued on the Dewey system.

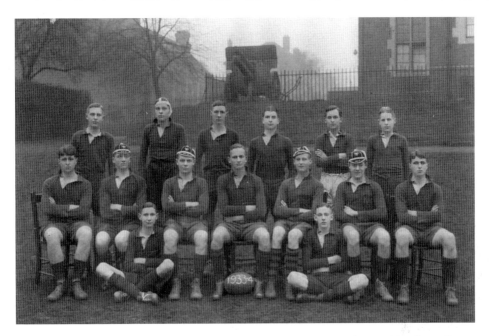

The 1933-34 Rugby First XV had a successful season, with nine wins, one draw and four losses. From left to right, back row: Alcock, Robertson, Washington, Hollinshead, Griffiths, Barlow. Seated: W. Brealey, G.L. Roscoe, Dolby, K.H. Roscoe, Bingham, Stevenson, P. Brealey. Front row: George, Boyd.

Dorothy Makinson and friends when she left the school in 1934: From left to right, back row: Dorothy Makinson, Dorothy Martin. Front row: Denise Dudley, Joan Martin (Hanley High School), Brenda Bennett, Edna Brown (now Edna Hallatt MBE). Edna has been a Governor at the schools for over fifty years.

The Orme Girls' annual Prize Distribution in the Municipal Hall, 1935. Seated, second left, is guest speaker Miss Vera Brittain, author of *Testament of Youth*. Vera explained that Miss Brittain was her pen name, and that she was proud to attend since she was both a native of Newcastle and a mother of two girls with strong views on the education girls should receive.

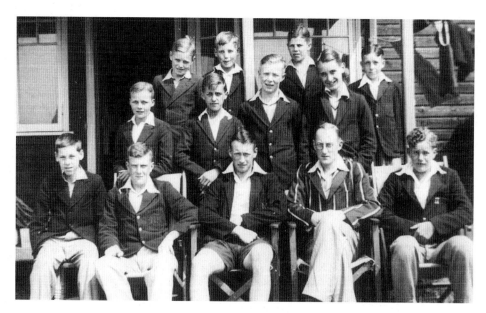

A.K. Barton organised High School visits to Croyde from 1935 to 1939. These included visits to local beauty spots, lighthouse tours and cricket matches. Barton taught at the school from 1934 to 1971. House Master for School House and Senior English Master from 1948, he was responsible for numerous school activities, such as the Debating and Literary Societies, the New Music Group and the Stamp Club. He also edited *The Fire-Fly* for a time.

In celebration of the 25th anniversary of the accession of King George V, the Mayor of Newcastle, J. Bentley, presented a souvenir book to every secondary school pupil in the borough. Each Orme Girl held their book while being addressed by Miss Sprunt and the mayor.

Oxford graduate Tom Stinton at the centre of the 1936 school photograph. He was appointed as the fourth High School headmaster in 1926. The *Fire-Fly* editorial following his retirement in 1948 records: 'To borrow a metaphor from his favourite game, Mr Stinton not only played a brilliant innings here, delighting hundreds of people, but has also left a magnificent pitch. May the next man in have as fine a score!'

Part of the New Building devoted to the Preparatory School in 1936. The Preparatory School, to which boys were admitted from age eight, had its first form on the top floor, and lower second and upper second forms downstairs. The boys had their own cloakroom and did not have to come into the main school – the Masters went to them. A further extension was added in 1967, back right, providing a new cloakroom, toilets and a classroom.

The start of the High School Annual Cross-Country run in Pilkington Avenue, the Westlands, in 1938. Watched by a large number of parents, 132 boys took part.

Opposite above: Miss Sprunt with the 1938 prefects. From left to right, back row: K. Dixon, C. Dudley, F. Boulton, M. Gilmore, M. Boulton, K. Seabridge. Seated: J. Harries, Miss Sprunt, D. Boyd. In the background is the 'temporary' annexe built in 1936, partly demolished in 1958 and finally demolished in the 1990s. During the 1936 alterations, middle school forms were placed on part-time attendance for five weeks.

Opposite below: On her retirement in July 1938 Miss Sprunt was presented with an album, signed by staff members, containing photographs of staff past and present. Pictured are some long-serving staff members, from left to right: Miss Harrison (1907-36), Miss Wood (1924-39), Miss Beard (1918-34), Miss Hopkirk (1892-1926), Miss Jenkinson (1908-43). In 1943, Miss Hopkirk's family funded Art books and an Art Prize in her memory.

Above: The quad in 1938 before alterations, as part of wider building work, which amalgamated the boarders' accommodation with the main High School buildings. Boarders were subsequently housed by Masters Dudley and Warne in their Lancaster Road houses.

Left: The dormitories were converted into a dining room, becoming classrooms in the 1990s. Other High School building work in summer 1938 provided new classrooms, an advanced laboratory, improved workshops, additional changing rooms and a new service kitchen. Also, the Memorial Hall was lengthened, with the new section panelled in oak to match the existing walls. The Bishop of Southwell (ON), who had dedicated the War Memorial in the Hall in 1923, officially opened the new facilities.

Above left: Miss Noël Paterson was Orme Girls' headmistress for four terms in 1938 and 1939, leaving to get married. Glebeland, acquired in 1932, provided this tennis court – now the site of the Pre-Preparatory and Nursery Department – air-raid shelters, hockey pitch and, briefly, vegetable gardens and shrubberies where lunchtime volunteers worked.

Above right: Dunbar Bishop (ON) chaired the Fundraising Committee launched in 1937 for a school swimming baths, formally opened by Sir Ernest Johnson (ON) in July 1938. The baths cost over £5,000, with the funds not fully raised until a two-day grand bazaar in 1939 raised in excess of £1,000.

A 1939 diving lesson being given by G. Clement DCM, the instructor at the swimming baths. In the holidays, the baths were open to past and present pupils. The Parogon Club was formed to encourage use of the baths by parents (PAR), Old Girls (OG) and Old Newcastilians (ON).

In his hymnbook, Gibson (front, second from right) recorded what became of each of the 1938 and 1939 praepostors. These included Fox (back, fourth from right), who drew the cartoon below. Typical of the time, many went on to serve with distinction during the Second World War, with Howson (top, second left) being awarded the Military Cross.

Pupil F.T. Fox's November 1939 cartoon, *As Others See Us*, depicted some of the High School staff. From left to right: F. Bacchus (taught at the school 1919-43), S.J. Smith (1927-70), G.H. Clough (1919-53), E. Warne (1929-46), D.L. Morris (1927-70), E. Dudley (1912-52), J.H. Taylor (1929-70), A.S. Horne (1931-69), W. Hancock (1922-50), J.W. Ashley-Smith (1936-41), A.K. Barton (1934-71), E.G. Collins (1930-62), J.P.C. Smith (1926-67) and seated G.F. Page (1914-49).

four

Renewal and Growth

War was once again the dominating influence in the 1940s. A number of Masters served during the Second World War, and fifty-one ONs lost their lives. Almost exactly ten years after the opening of the New Buildings, the Orme Girls' School was damaged in an air raid. Three incendiary bombs hit the school in November 1940, leaving damaged floorboards and holes in the roof and ceiling of a classroom and the gymnasium. The tennis court was also damaged. Thankfully, substantial damage was avoided by the prompt action of staff and the fire service.

John Barrington Wain, author and Professor of Poetry at Oxford, in his school uniform in 1942. He attended the High School from 1935 to 1942. In addition to success with novels, especially *The Contenders* which has been translated into several languages, he wrote a long story in verse and three volumes of short poems. He was also a renowned critic, praised for his powers of balanced criticism.

The inspection by Mrs H.C. Wenger, accompanied by the Mayor and Company Commander Miss Duggan, at a rally of the Girls' Training Corp held at the Orme in 1943. Three GTC companies in Newcastle trained and prepared girls for all three services, with one company based at the school. Members included both pupils and Old Girls.

Opposite above: Corporal Taylor demonstrating grenade throwing to High School Junior Training Corp (JTC) members, including Sherratt, Lawton, Espley, Rhead, Wain, Oldham, Peters and Steele. Under the direction of their Masters, the entire school had days off to assemble gas masks for the town of Newcastle.

Opposite below: The newly built swimming baths form a backdrop for the 1941 sack race. The two-day finals of the High School Athletic Sports at the end of the spring term were marred by inclement weather, 'rendering the efforts of the timekeepers almost entirely a work of supererogation' (*The Fire-Fly*, June 1941). Miss Kemp, newly appointed Orme Girls' headmistress, distributed the prizes in the Memorial Hall.

The High School supported a Junior Training Corp, including its own band. In 1944, the JTC held its first annual camp for five years. About forty cadets and NCOs attended under the command of Captain J.P.C. Smith and Second Lieutenant A.E. Collins. A visit to an American Army camp was included, helping the boys to learn about the discipline, equipment and training of an American soldier.

Through the Ship Adoption Society, the schools adopted the 320ft-long steam-driven Merchant Navy vessel SS *Flamma*. On 8 February 1944, Captain Mordue addressed the High School in the Memorial Hall and thanked all who had written and sent gifts to the ship's crew. He presented a silver challenge cup to the Head of School, M.N. Garvey. This Mordue Cup was to be awarded annually to the winner of some event in sports.

Captain Mordue also visited the Orme Girls' and presented the SS *Flamma* Cup, to be awarded to the winner of a handicapped competition for the fastest individual swimmer. He handed over a plaque of the Merchant Navy crest and a photograph of the ship, and issued an invitation to both schools to visit the ship whenever it was in port. Miss Kemp and Head Girl Christine Robson are alongside the captain.

A large crowd gathered for a bonfire on the High School grounds, one of many celebrations for VE Day in May 1945.

Left: One impact of the war on the High School was the arrival of female teachers in 1941. This 1945 charcoal and chalk sketch is one of many drawn by one such teacher, Nora Grisenthwaite, an Oxford graduate who was appointed to teach English, Art and History. The sketch is of eleven-year-old Graham Forrester, who went on to become Head of School.

Below: The Old Girls' Association's seventieth birthday cake – designed by Mr Hanford, made by Miss Sibbald and painted by Miss Bennett. Over 200 Old Girls, staff and prefects listened to speeches by Miss Kemp, Mrs Myott and Kathleen Holding (head girl). Miss Kemp said 'that seventy years is the allotted span of man's life, but in the life of a girls' school it is but a beginning'.

Right: As part of the seventieth birthday celebrations, the girls performed Sheridan's *The Rivals* in the Memorial Hall in May 1946. Miss Follows produced it, and the stage manager was Miss Welland. Mr Taylor, assisted by High School pupils, provided lighting, etc. and Miss Witton and school friends the music. From left to right: Pauline Lovatt, Sheila Smith, Margaret Walton.

Below: A party of twenty-one Dutch boys and girls, aged eight to fourteen, including some orphans, spent two months in the borough recuperating from privations suffered during the war. On arrival in June 1946, the mayor and mayoress welcomed them. The girls attended the Orme Girls' and took part in all activities – including a party at Lewis's and visits to Chester and Rhyl.

Above: The first High School play for nine years was *Treasure Island*, performed in December 1946. Fourteen people were in the cast, but forty boys were involved. From left to right, back row: Yates, Whittow, Hurst, Hewitt, Till, Warren, Griffiths, Turner. Front row: Leigh, Whitehurst, Watkin, Woolliscroft, Nixon, Pearson, Perry. Till was praised for making Long John Silver 'the hard-hearted old pirate captain he was without committing the obvious sin of over-acting'.

Left: Miss Griffiths, who taught PE at the Orme Girls' from 1945 to 1952, leaving Upper St Paul's in the 1940s. She also taught gymnastics and swimming at the High School.

A dance was held in the Memorial Hall during a visit by Dutch pupils in 1947. Headmistress Miss de Bruyne accompanied girls from her school near Leeuwarden, Friesland. Orme Girls' pupils went to Holland on an exchange visit in the following year.

Miss Eckstein teaching in the Annexe in 1948. She taught German and Latin at the Orme Girls' and was in charge of the Charities Account. The Prefects' Minutes record that some of the Lower IVs had been doing somersaults on the Annexe veranda. The picture includes Gillian Norbury, Rosemary Chapman (standing), Jean Day and Betty Timmis.

A professional photographer from Wimbledon took, for export, a series of photographs of the girls working and playing in the school. Miss Tunnicliffe (left), Head of Science, led a 1948 Chemistry demonstration in what is now part of Orme House. She taught at the Orme Girls' from 1939 to 1965 and was Acting Head for sixteen months during the ill health of Miss Kemp and prior to Miss Smith's arrival.

VA Form Mistress 1948-49, Miss Allison taught Physics, Chemistry, Games and Scripture from 1943 to 1949. Cynthia Smart (front, third from left) was later head girl. After completing a degree at Oxford, Cynthia taught Classics at the school for thirty-five years.

In the spring term of 1948 the Orme Girls' staff performed *The Rose and the Ring*, produced by Miss Welland, in the Victoria Library. Staff on the steps leading up to the Victoria Road entrance include Misses Slater, Kemp, Bennett, Stanway, Lewis, Wylie, Ray and Wells, and Mr Butler.

The 1948 third year VI. History teacher Miss Cowe (back row, fourth from left) was in charge of the Orme Girls' during Miss Sprunt's leave of absence in 1937. Miss Rowley (back row, sixth from left), motto 'Perfection, nothing less', taught French. Both taught at the school from 1928 to 1948.

Arnold Bennett's niece, Ruth Bennett (left), was a pupil at the Orme Girls' from 1919 to 1927, and needlework teacher from 1939 to 1970. Between them, Ruth and her mother, who was also a pupil, knew every Orme Girls' headmistress. Ruth has long been actively involved in the Old Girls' Society.

Senior and Junior Prefects, 1948-49. The Senior Prefects (seated, left to right) are Mary Bowdler, Gwynneth Timmis, Joan Shepherd, Ann Page and Alwyn Clough. Mary Bowdler returned to the Orme Girls' in 1974 to teach Domestic Science. Prefects' Minutes books record issues such as 'girls not wearing their hats and, when they do, having tucks in them all the way round'.

First organised in 1940 as part of the war effort, a Harvest Camp at Bromyard continued for twenty years, largely organised by Mathematics Master D.L. Morris (second from left) and caretaker T. White. In 1949, the boys were visited by the Bishop of Hereford (sixth from left) who was 'very much impressed by the excellent record of work carried out by the camp over the past nine years'.

The first post-war Arts and Science Exhibition was held over two days in 1949 and was regarded as the most successful the High School had arranged. The Memorial Hall exhibits included paintings, etchings, sculpture and pottery. The senior boys demonstrated experiments in the Science Wing.

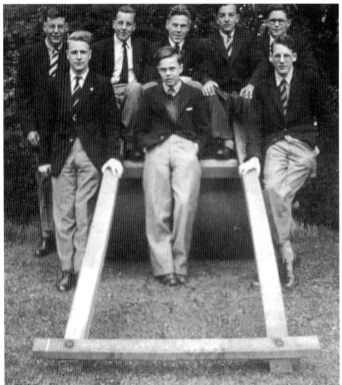

Above: Lord Webb Johnson (centre) distributed the prizes at the High School Speech Day and Prize Giving in 1950. Former President of the Royal College of Surgeons and surgeon to Queen Mary, Webb Johnson attended the school from 1890-97, when he was a member of the Rugby XV. He announced that he would donate £100 to the ONs War Memorial fund for the erection of a cricket pavilion on Stubbs Field.

Left: Upper VI Science pupils in summer 1950. From left to right, back row: Bickell, Thompson, Wilson, Gribbin, Swift. Front row: Smith, Stubbs, Cross.

Above: In 1949–50, Upper III Alpha travelled by bus to Sheldon House, a Dr Barnado's home in Shrewsbury. The children, aged ten months to six years, gave them an 'uproarious welcome' – older children had gone to school. After lunch on the lawn, the Orme Girls' went for a walk in the grounds and down to the River Severn.

Right: Having taught at the High School since 1912, Oxford and Sorbonne-educated Edmund Dudley was Second Master when he retired in 1952. His wife also taught at the High School in 1918. Their five daughters attended the Orme Girls'. The headmaster's house can be seen in the background.

To mark the Orme Girls' seventy-sixth birthday, parents were invited to an Open Day in July 1952. The day included a gymnastic display on the field, the House Tennis Tournament, dancing displays and a parade of prefects wearing the 1878 uniform – plus free ice cream and biscuits. Different aspects of schoolwork were displayed in the Studio, Room 5 and in the form rooms.

Opposite: Jim Todd with his staff in 1952. An Oxford graduate, Jim was headmaster at the High School from 1948 to 1963. The grey suit worn by boys until 2004 was introduced during this time. On leaving, he became Secretary to the Oxford University Delegacy for the Inspection and Examination of Schools, and Oxford Secretary to the Oxford and Cambridge Schools' Examination Board.

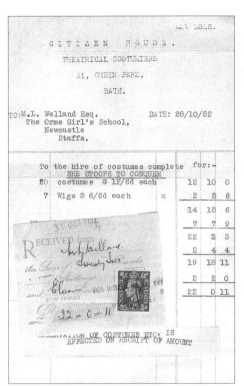

CITIZEN HOUSE.

THEATRICAL COSTUMIERS

21, GREEN PARK,

BATH.

TO: M.L. Welland Esq.   DATE: 28/10/52
     The Orme Girl's School,
     Newcastle
     Staffs.

To the hire of costumes complete for:-
     SHE STOOPS TO CONQUER
20 costumes @ 12/6d each   12 10 0
7   Wigs @ 6/6d each   m   2   5 6
                                   14 15 6
                                    7   7 9
                                   22   3 3
                                    2   4 4
                                   19 18 11
                                    2   2 0
                                   22   0 11

RECEIVED FOR

the Sum of Twenty Two Pounds

and Eleven   FOR OIT   S
WITH THANKS

£ 22 - 0 - 11

RENOVATION OF COSTUMES ETC. IS
EFFECTED ON RECEIPT OF AMOUNT

Left: Theatrical costumes for *She Stoops to Conquer* cost £22 in 1952.

Below: She Stoops to Conquer performers, St Paul's, Christmas 1952. The new stage curtains, mainly funded by the Parents' Association, were used for the first time. Eileen Topham (now Mrs Chamberlain – middle, second left) returned to teach English and was the producer for many school plays. At the end of the summer term in 1996, June Yates (now Mrs Lovatt – front, third left) retired as Head of Girls' Physical Education after twenty-eight years.

A.K. Barton took Form VC to the Barlaston Wedgwood factory in 1952.

The Orme Girls' Prize Giving, 1953, in the Municipal Hall. Professor Peel, Professor of Education and Head of Department at the University of Birmingham, presented the prizes.

About seventy members and guests attended the 1953 ON Annual Dinner at the Castle Hotel, Newcastle. G.W. Huntbach, the City Coroner and ON President, is standing in the centre of the head table with the Mayor of Newcastle. On Huntbach's left is chief guest Professor F.A. Vick OBE, Vice-Principal of the University College of North Staffordshire.

The presentation of three seats to the High School to commemorate the Coronation of Queen Elizabeth II in 1953.

Opposite below: The High School Hockey Team in 1954. From left to right, back row: Purcell, Sutton, Barnett, Stevenson, Smart, Sutton, Smith. Front row: Fishwick, Winkle, Lancaster, Talbot, Green. Goalkeeper Fishwick played for England, and in the Great Britain team at both the Rome and Tokyo Olympics.

At the January 1954 Old Girls' Dinner, Miss Elnith Kemp, headmistress from January 1940 to December 1951, was presented with a portrait of herself. She in turn donated it to the school. On her retirement, Miss Kemp also donated the flowering trees that can still be seen along the top edge of the playing field, bordering Victoria Road. From left to right: Edna Hallatt, Sydney Myott, Ronald Ford, Elnith Kemp, Sheila Smith.

The War Memorial Pavilion, built for the school by the ONs, was dedicated on the tenth anniversary of D-Day, June 1955. J.H.D. Myatt (ON), who had managed the War Memorial Fund, formally opened the Pavilion. The clock was the gift of E.D. Dennis, ON.

In addition to the staff and pupils, over 200 parents and ONs witnessed the opening of the War Memorial Pavilion.

Opposite above: In April 1956, cadets attended a gliding course at Meir. All of them made about forty flights, including three solo flights. During the year, the RAF section of the CCF had grown in numbers and in the subjects covered.

Opposite below: A tennis tournament, pupils against Old Girls, was organised as part of the Orme Girls' eightieth birthday celebrations in 1956. From left to right, pupils Barbara Redfern and Rosemary Collier, and Old Girls Nora Whalley and Ann Hilton.

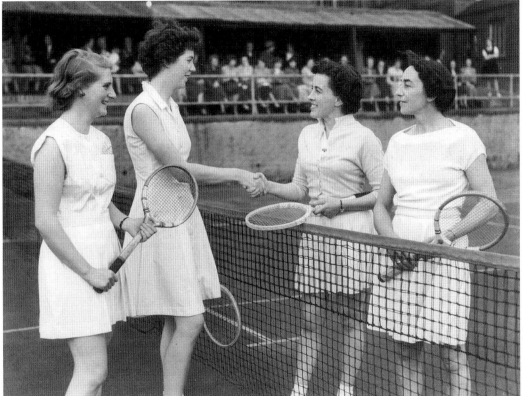

Left: For the eightieth birthday celebrations, pupils entertained the Old Girls with a display of country dancing, organised by Mrs Kirkwood and Miss Wordsworth. Mary Brockbank, Susan Halliwell and Sheila Glover are among the performers. The tree outside the gymnasium has since been removed.

Below: Members of the Orme Girls' Photographic Society in 1957. In light of the large numbers at this time, Miss Tunnicliffe gave up two dinner hours per week to supervise the meetings. The dark rooms were at the back of the chemistry laboratory. An annual competition was held at the end of the summer term. The society also took form photographs, which were sold to the girls.

It's my idea of a reply to those boaters, sir,"

Above: Miss Smith recorded for 1 May 1958 that 'The school wore boaters for the first time. The summer hat in pre-war days was a panama. It was discontinued during the war'. The boaters were available from Henry Whites for 24s 11d.

Left: The *Sentinel* also recorded the introduction of boaters!

Above: High School pupils in the new Science Wing in 1959. Colonel Sir George Wade MC, ON, who officially opened this on Founders' Day twelve months earlier, had spoken of the many and increasing opportunities available in the field of science. In the previous year, four Oxford and Cambridge science scholarships had been gained.

Right: Sir George Wade launched the Harrison–Stinton Memorial Appeal with the aim of raising £25,000 to provide further buildings; this was because the High School was now educating 650 boys. The initial building was designed to house 150 boys and when the New Building was added in 1930, there were 330 boys.

Opposite above: The official opening of the extension to the New Buildings at the Orme Girls' by the Revd H.M. Connop Price in July 1958. In addition to Governors and the architect, Mr Oldacre, a large number of parents and pupils attended. The ceremony was held out of doors and was followed by a summer concert in the Victoria Library. Orme House now occupies the New Buildings.

Opposite below: A group of girls attempted to stop Keele University students who, as part of their 1959 Rag Week, were trying to 'borrow' the Crimean cannon from Stubbs Walk. Later, however, the cannon appeared as part of the Rag Week procession.

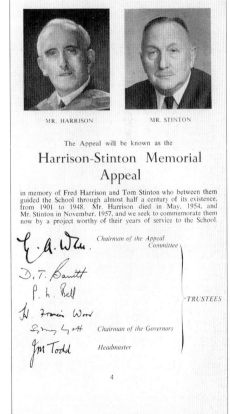

MR. HARRISON   MR. STINTON

The Appeal will be known as the

Harrison-Stinton Memorial Appeal

in memory of Fred Harrison and Tom Stinton who between them guided the School through almost half a century of its existence, from 1901 to 1948. Mr. Harrison died in May, 1954, and Mr. Stinton in November, 1957, and we seek to commemorate them now by a project worthy of their years of service to the School.

Chairman of the Appeal Committee

TRUSTEES

Chairman of the Governors

Headmaster

4

The trees donated by Miss Kemp are along the Victoria Road, top left in this 1959 view of the schools. The Orme Girls' paid Aerofilms of Elstree £13 to supply aerial photographs.

The first year in which pupils rang the bells of St Giles' Church for Founders' Day was 1959. The bellringers include Erica Kisch and Claire Bickell. While they came together to ring on Founders' Day, the girls were active ringers at different churches in the area. St Giles' bells have since been rung for Founders' Day on many occasions.

five

Success and Celebration

The schools flourished and continued to expand in the relative affluence of the 1960s and 1970s, cementing their reputation among Staffordshire's finest schools. The School Centenaries were also celebrated in this period, with the visit of HRH Princess Margaret to the High School providing a highlight.

Under the captaincy of I.T.F. Rowe (sixth from the left) all 1959-60 High School cross-country matches were won. The undefeated record lasted from September 1958 until December 1962, seventy matches in all. On the far right is Dr Doug Eyles who was at the school from 1948 to 1974. During this time, his coaching produced both national and Olympic athletes.

In April 1960 a party of Orme Girls' pupils, accompanied by Miss Fraser, Miss Barnett and Miss Ellsmore, travelled to Wengern Alp. From left to right: Anne Green, Pat Knowles, Carolyn West, Beris Hazeldine, Lesley Mee, ski instructor, Julia Hackney, Julie Lovatt, Kay Smith, Avril Evans.

The Orme Girls' staff in 1960. Miss Smith (front row centre) was headmistress from January 1952 to July 1969. She wrote a short history of the school, published in 1961. While at the school, she kept a diary recording school events, including newspaper cuttings. Personal observations and details were included, and invariably a note about the weather for outdoor events!

The Orme Girls' Swimming Team won the Senior Cup in the 1960 Newcastle Schools' Swimming Gala. The school took the first two places in the two-length back crawl, with the winner, Sheila Thornley (centre right), being congratulated here by runner-up Jean Brockbank.

Above: The Orme Girls' raised £200 for World Refugee Year, which ended in 1960. They gathered in the Victoria Library where a cheque was presented to Councillor Ford, Chairman of the Newcastle Education Committee. Deputy Head Girl Erica Kisch gave Councillor Ford a small piece of pottery that had been made in school.

Left: One of the oldest Old Newcastilians, local solicitor Harry Poole, was Clerk to the Governors from 1917 until his death, aged ninety-five, on Christmas Eve 1961. In 1954, Harry was presented with a portrait of himself to mark the eightieth anniversary of the school buildings – he could recall being taken as a boy to see the school being built. His son, J.D. Poole, replaced him as Clerk to the Governors.

As part of the eighty-fifth birthday celebrations, the Old Girls held a dinner at the Castle Hotel. Three generations of former pupils were present. The speaker was Miss Barnes, member of staff from 1916-29. Amy Vaughan Jones, who was at the school at the beginning of the century, proposed a vote of thanks.

Sydney Myott, ON, was Mayor of Newcastle three times and a Governor at the schools for fifty-three years, twenty as Chairman. He laid the Sydney Myott Foundation Stone for a new block (now M Block) to house two laboratories, four classrooms and a preparation room. Headmistress Miss Smith recorded in her diary that 'it was a showery day, but the sun shone for the outdoor part of the ceremony'.

Junior girls, some of nearly 600 pupils who cheered as eighty-nine-year-old Mr Myott laid the foundation stone of the new block named in his honour.

The annual inter-house cross-country race in 1962. In the junior race, the first three – Leigh (fifteen minutes and forty-two seconds), Ward and Hand – all beat the previous year's record time. Lear won the senior event in twenty-three minutes and thirty-four seconds, just two seconds outside Austin's record time. Billington was second and Mills third.

Opposite above: The 1962 Orme Girls' Prize Giving was held in the King's Hall, Stoke. Invitations were issued to one parent per girl, and both parents of prize-winners and Upper VI girls.

Opposite below: Upper IV Latin, 1962. From left to right, back row: Doreen Griffin, Pamela Dale, Margaret Chapman, Susan Griffiths, Jennifer Gibbs, Gillian Beresford, Barbara Chainey, Elizabeth Keeling, Margaret Hinks. Third row: Mary Stock, Janet Riley, Diana Rhodes, Angela West, Susan Minshall, Celia Riley, Pat Brownsword. Second row: Madeleine McCallion, Judith Foskett, Barbara Dutton, Anne McBratney, Mrs Sorrell (English), Judith Bettelley, Sheila Ramage, Claire Pickford, Margaret Dinnick. Front row: Lynne Stokes, Anne Fox, Helen Renshaw, Caroline Stewart, Jacqueline Davies, Jacqueline Mee, Pat Mills.

The first joint Orme Girls' and High School production was *Macbeth* in 1963. The Royal Shakespeare Theatre provided costumes. There were seven female parts, with Cherith Davenport as Lady Macbeth. Dulson played Macbeth. A reviewer suggested Miss Macphail was invaluable to the witches in particular, who, under her guidance, 'cackled so well'.

Miss Smith's diary, July 1963: 'Sports Day and fine!' Miss Moon took this photograph as part of a series recording Orme Girls' events during the school year.

Above: The 1963-64 High School Hockey Team was the most successful in the school's history, being undefeated throughout the season. From left to right, standing: Goodwin, Rowley, Clowes, Higson, Whittaker, Mr Carr. Seated: Thomas, Bassett, Toft (captain), Lewis, Prophett. Thomas and Lewis both had final trials for the Welsh Schoolboys at Cardiff. Len Bassett later became a Governor at the school and was elected Chair in 2004.

Right: Ernest Warrilow, ON, photographed Albert John Victor Roberts on his arrival as headmaster in 1964. A well-known local historian and *Sentinel* photographer, Warrilow was for many years the main contributor of the pictures contained in *The Fire-Fly*. Roberts resigned in 1972 to become headmaster of the Tiffin School. While at the High School, he introduced a five-day week.

Boys assembled in the quadrangle for the 1964 opening of the £24,000 High School extensions by Dr Harold Taylor, Vice-Chancellor of Keele University. Mary Stinton, wife of the former headmaster, laid the foundation stone for the first section of the new extension in 1963. She used the same gavel as King George IV had when laying the foundation stone for the 1829 restoration of Windsor Castle.

A Christmas card was produced showing the new Harrison Stinton Science Block, drawn by Major N.J. Dobbin, High School Head of Art. He taught at the school from 1962 to 1981 and was associated with the CCF throughout this time, becoming Officer Commanding in 1972.

Netball's First VII was unbeaten by any other school team in 1964-65. From left to right: Susan Heywood, Ann Robinson, Anne McBratney, Jennifer Gibbs, Susan Minshall, Margaret Varnam, Anne Steele. During the year, three of the team (McBratney, Minshall, Steele) were among five girls who qualified to umpire club standard matches.

A High School visit to Russia was organised in 1964 by Masters Norris (centre, white suit) and Cross. The ship's first port of call was Copenhagen. Visits included Lenin's embalmed body, Peter the Great's Summer Palace and the Moscow State University. A mistake by the Soviet travel agency meant spending an unscheduled day in West Berlin and arriving home twenty-four hours late.

Pre-service training unit members on parade for the 1965 Newcastle CCF inspection. The inspecting officer was Colonel Miller, Commanding Officer of Mercian Brigade. He congratulated the cadets on a first-class effort. On parade were fifty-one Army, twenty-seven RAF and thirty-two PSU cadets. High School caps were a familiar sight at this time.

First World War veteran Albert Clay, aged seventy-four, retired in 1965 after working for forty-two years as a High School caretaker. He received an inscribed wallet containing a cheque from Head Boy Christopher Stoddard in the presence of Headmaster John Roberts and other staff members.

An Orme Girls' Parents Association film show in November 1967. Mr H.O. Wardell (projectionist) presented an interesting programme of colour films, which were both entertaining and instructive. Also present was Parents Association Chairman Mr G. Oldacre.

Head Boy Henry Edwin Salt QC attended the school from 1911 to 1916. In 1967, he presented an armorial window to match the Kitchener Window in the Memorial Hall, both of which can be seen at the back of the stage. Salt served in the First World War and was a distinguished academic at Cambridge. He both taught and practised law, and was Chancellor of the County Palatine of Durham 1960-69.

VIRGINIA MORRIS RUTH OPPENHEIMER KATHLEEN MACHIN LINDSAY GOUGH

The Orme Girls' team was defeated by just one mark in Anglia Television's 1969 wildlife quiz game *Survival*. Guided by Miss Wyke, the four team members and reserve (Alison Morrey) had to learn as much as they could about the cat family, both real and fictional. One of the questions answered incorrectly was about *Growl Tiger* – only Alison had read T.S. Elliott's *Practical Cats*!

Opposite, above: An ON team beat the High School Cricket Team in the Founders' Day match, June 1969. In the centre are the captains, K. Lovewell and M. Fairbanks.

Opposite, below: Second from the right on the front row is Mrs Freda Barlow – subsequently Buxton – at her first Prize Giving as headmistress in 1969. She was headmistress for eleven years. In her address, she explained that she wanted the girls to leave the school not educated – which implied something finite – but educable. The important thing was to have an open mind to receive the wealth of experience and ideas that pour in with each day of living.

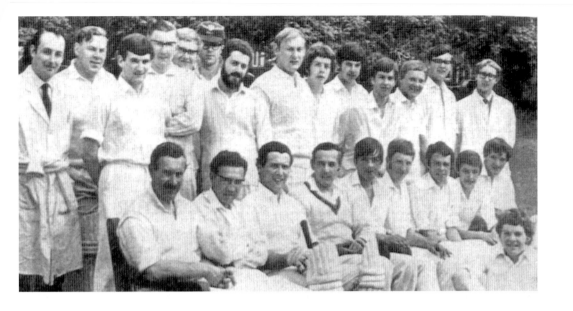

Sir David T. Barritt, ON, Chairman of Governors, officially opened the new tennis courts at the High School in July 1969. With him is Headmaster John Roberts. A mixed doubles competition involving the Orme Girls' was played following the opening, won by Brigit Youell, Captain OGS, and R.J. Whitehouse, NHS.

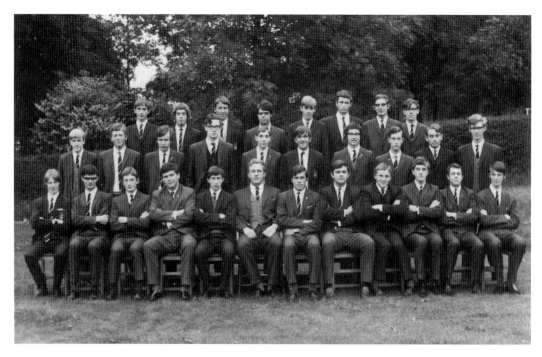

In the centre of the 1969-70 Praepostors is Peter Scragg (with waistcoat), Head Boy and Chairman of the Social Action Group. This group worked closely with the Junior Council of Social Service and helped to organise events such as a sponsored walk for the Friends of Bradwell Hospital, a firework display at May Place Children's Home and carol singing.

Mrs Buxton with the mayor and mayoress at an Orme Girls' Open Day in October 1970. Various activities were on view including a PE display, junior Science and a range of projects. Jill Lidstone, from the Victoria Theatre, led a practical Drama class.

The first High School Rugby XV to play abroad won the Michelin Tournament at Bad Kreuznach in 1971. Courtesy of Michelin, other junior XVs also travelled to West Germany and played against German, French and Belgian teams. From left to right: Lamb, Brown, Coulombeau, Cartwright, Gray and Owen (captain). Ian Cartwright returned to teach at the school in 1981 and became Director of Admissions in 2003.

Above: Captained by Janette Forrester, the 1971-72 Under-18 Netball Team had their most successful season ever, winning a series of tournaments but narrowly losing in the final of the National Schools Competition. Kathryn Jones played goal attack for the Under-19 England Schoolgirls while Christine Moss was a travelling reserve.

Left: The Orme Girls' 1973 'Evening of Light Entertainment with Songs From the Shows' included extracts from *The King & I*. Ruth Parker (left) was Head Girl in 1974/75.

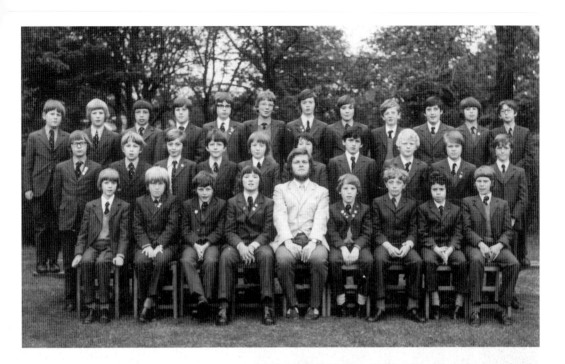

Above: History Master Peter Shilston with his 1973-74 Form, 1 Alpha. Peter was a *Mastermind* contestant in 1981. He taught at the school for nineteen years and, among many other contributions, started the school bookshop for the sale of new and second-hand books.

Right: Princess Margaret visited the High School during the centenary celebrations. Max Hunt, Head of History, showed Her Royal Highness extracts from the archives. Max also presented her with a specially bound No. 1 copy of his book, *Newcastle High School 1874-1974*. Paperback versions of the book were sold for 70p each.

The centenary staff. From left to right, back row: Love, Rhodes, Benson, Blake, Hall, Leech, Hartshorne, Goodwin, Nussey, Bagguley, Dobbin, Wilson, Royal. Middle row: Chappell, James, Maxfield, Shilston, Williams, Brown, Wetherby, Jones, Price, Mitra, Jones. Front row: Swift, Parrack, Norris, Stretch, Tams, Hampson, Barnes, Brookes, Eyles, Hadfield, Collis, Hunt, Jackson. Reg Brookes (front row, sixth from right) was acting headmaster between 1972 and 1974.

Opposite above: Princess Margaret unveiled the Centenary Plaque above the Mount Pleasant entrance to the school. The foundation stone and all the stonework on the old building were cleaned in preparation for the centenary year.

Opposite below: Headmaster Bill Donaldson recorded in his centenary year report: 'The ground staff have planted a hundred trees as part of the centenary programme. ... A cherry tree has been planted in the circular flowerbed at the main entrance to the school, thus restoring the appearance to what it was at the time of the 1874 etching'. The Chairman of Governors is planting the hundredth tree with the Head Boy, Richard Owen, looking on. Tom White (far right) was school caretaker from 1931 to 1974.

J.W. (Bill) Donaldson became headmaster at the end of the centenary year. Charged with leading the school into independence, he became Newcastle-under-Lyme School's first principal in 1982, retiring in 1990. Seven of the staff appointed in the period went on to headships in other independent schools.

In the 1970s, Orion, Gemini and Scorpio, based on the Orme Girls' School initials, replaced the girls' York, Lancaster, Tudor, Stuart and Norman Houses. Forms were grouped in houses and named according to them. The first new house captains were, from left to right: Sheena Beech (Orion), Cheryl Whitehouse (Scorpio), Anita Lindop (Gemini), Gillian Ray (Scorpio), Susan Walley (Gemini), Caroline Abbot (Orion).

Watched by Head Girl Jill Shaw (second left) and others in the Victoria Library, former pupil and Chairman of Governors Dr Joan Acheson unveiled a plaque marking the Orme Girls' centenary in 1976. It cost £134 and includes a coat of arms, shield, scroll and motto painted in gilt.

With some in Victorian dress, the school gathered on the tennis court to watch Amelia Taylor cut the Centenary Cake that Mary Bowdler had made. At ninety, Amelia was the oldest Old Girl in the district. She was head girl when Oliver Lodge opened the library in 1908 and was a classmate of Marjorie Whitfield, later Mrs Sidney Myott.

As part of the centenary celebrations, over 300 girls and twenty staff (half the school), went on a five-day visit to Holland. The various activities included trips to The Hague, the Holland in Miniature exhibition, the Aalsmeer flower auctions and a windmill museum. The group stayed at a Dutch Youth Hostel.

High School pupils leaving St Giles' Church after the Founders' Day Service in June 1977. Head Boy N. Tawney read a lesson from John Chapter 13. A collection for the Queen's Silver Jubilee Appeal and Save the Children raised £100.

The combined orchestras and choirs of the High School and Orme Girls' at the Victoria Hall gave a concert in 1978. The programme (2p) included a selection of madrigals and works by Mozart, Handel, Purcell and Beethoven. The conductors, Gillian Ryder and Geoffrey Walker, were both ex-pupils who had returned as music teachers.

Janet MacKay (right) in the Science laboratory with Christine Holloway. Janet was one of two girls who, in 1978, first sat five A-Levels, and the first to achieve five A grades. She went on to study Medicine at Trinity College Cambridge – being among the first women to enter Trinity. Janet's brothers Robert and David went to the High School and Trinity.

Form tutor Bill Gillen asked the sixth-formers requiring a copy of this 1979 form photograph to sign their names on a list. As a result, sixteen signatures are now in the school archives. Gillen was Head of English, leaving in 1980 to become deputy head of the Royal Grammar School, Guildford.

Opposite above: One long-established Orme Girls' tradition is the annual Dance Competition. This is Form VS in the Victoria site gymnasium in 1979. From left to right, back row: Helen Wareham, Lynda Simpson, Sarah Farrington, Caroline Pettitt, Julie Buckley. Front row: Karen Broomhall, Heather McIntosh.

Opposite below: In 1966, Marie Goodwin (centre, behind golf trolley) founded the Old Girls' Golf Society, who now compete annually for the Marie Goodwin Trophy. The 1979 match between the Old Newcastilians, led by their captain Denis Tams DFC (front), and Old Girls was won by the ONs, 3½ to 2½. Tams taught ceramics at the school, retiring in 1981 after thirty-one years of service.

Sixth-former Jane Rogers won an all-expenses-paid trip to California in 1979 for research into the arts. This was first prize in a national competition with 17,000 entries. Alan Lucas, local manager of the sponsor, Lloyds Bank, presented Jane with a book, *Beautiful California*, and Headmistress Mrs Buxton with a giant cheque for £250. Christine Bradley won a second prize of £50 and six other girls received third place awards.

The Orme Girls' Art Room, where the walls regularly had murals added by the girls. Art is now taught in the Barratt Centre.

As early as 1911, *The Fire-Fly* recorded that golf 'has taken a deep root in the school'. The 1980-81 High School team was particularly successful. Guided by coach Denis Tams, Tim Beresford, David Gilford and Martin Keates won the 1981 Midlands Area Aer Lingus golf tournament for schools. David Gilford went on to become a professional golfer, and played against the USA in the 1991 and 1995 Ryder Cups.

A large number of photographs were taken for potential inclusion in the first Newcastle-under-Lyme School prospectus. These photographs captured many aspects of school life, including extra-curricular activities as well as, for example, language lessons.

Above: Mrs Buxton and the Orme Girls' staff prior to her retirement in 1980.

Left: Appointed in 1980, Hilary Ludlam was the last headmistress of the Orme Girls'. She was closely involved in the creation of Orme House, referring to the pupils as the 'Red Brigade'. A concert at the end of her final term included the surprise singing of a carol she had composed when a schoolgirl.

six

Newcastle-under-Lyme School

In 1981, the combined schools became independent with the creation of Newcastle-Under-Lyme School. Having passed the entrance examination, 220 new fee-paying pupils arrived, including seventy-three on the Government's Assisted Places Scheme. Fees were £395 per term. Substantial challenges have subsequently been faced, not least of which was the change of Government policy that ended the Assisted Places Scheme. However, under the leadership of successive principals and Governors, the school has flourished and now includes both a successful Preparatory Department, with Orme House opening in 1982, and a purpose-built Pre-Preparatory and Nursery Department opened in 2004. This now enables the school to offer education and care throughout the whole of a pupil's education years, from age three to eighteen.

There were initially two heads, Bill Donaldson and Hilary Ludlam, seen here welcoming some of the first pupils. In 1982, Bill Donaldson was appointed as the first principal of Newcastle-under-Lyme School.

Languages teacher Keith 'Ecka' Stretch retired as Group Scout Leader in 1981, ending his twenty-five-year association with the school Scout Troop. Past Scouts from all over the country watched Mrs Hood, Chairman of the Scout Parents Association, present Ecka with a silver salver and Black & Decker Workmate. When he died, the school Scouts used his bequest to purchase Ecka's Wood – an area of mature woodland near Stafford that the Scouts regularly visit.

The music accompanying the school's 1982 production of *A Midsummer Night's Dream* was composed, arranged and conducted by sixth-former Edward Derbyshire – even though he regarded music as a hobby!

The Preparatory Department, Orme House, opened in 1982. Ann Stamper, the first Head of Orme House, and class teacher Mabel Yeomans are with the first intake. The pupils are wearing the new uniform, which Mrs Ludlam chose. This included a tie designed by Art teacher Mr Hanford.

In 1932, the Orme Girls' acquired the 'Houses' Glenelg and Elmhurst, with a view to refurbishment. However, an architect's quotation suggested renovation would cost £100 but did not 'justify the expenditure involved'. A family continued to occupy Elmhurst until 1935. It was subsequently adapted to form three flats for members of staff, paying an annual rent of £60. The 'houses' were finally refurbished in 1982 to accommodate Orme House, and are now used by the Mathematics Department.

In 1983, Handel's *Messiah* was performed in the Victoria Hall by the girls' and boys' choirs, the Senior Orchestra, staff and members of the public who had responded to an advertisement seeking singers. The performance was the first time the 360 performers had come together.

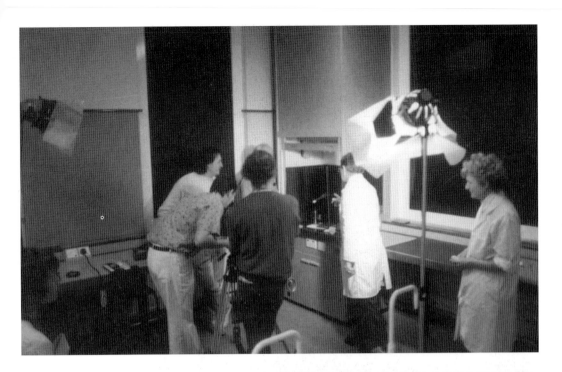

Above: Gordon Collis being filmed with Senior Laboratory Technician Audrey Gunstone. Gordon, Head of Science, was the Science Adviser for two secondary school series made by Granada Television in the mid-1980s, *Chemistry in Action* and *Science in Focus*.

Right: David Mackay (front left), was the first pupil to be awarded six A-Level A grades. While a sixth former he represented the UK at the 1985 International Physics Olympiad in Yugoslavia. Of 100 contestants from twenty countries, he was placed first in the practical examinations. In 2000, David was awarded a Fellowship of the Royal Society and became Professor of Natural Philosophy at Cambridge in 2003 – where brother Robert was also a professor.

Miss Hulse, English teacher at the school for over thirteen years, with her form in 1985. The building in the background is where Orme House is now situated.

Orme House pupils spent five days at Llangrannog in May 1986, at a cost of £63 each. Day trips and activities were organised, with a fancy dress party on the last evening. Sarah Donaldson (the principal's wife) is pictured with her group.

The gymnasium was transformed into the Lancaster site library in 1986, providing a significant increase in accommodation for pupils and study material. Kitchener's original desk is in the library.

The school tradition of winning sports honours continued with the 1987 Staffordshire winners of the Lord Taverners' Colts Competition. Skipper Mark Foster is holding the cup on the bat presented to him as Man of the Match. Matthew Colclough (back, third from left) represented England at Under-15 level.

Michèle Lainé was one of eight finalists in the televised 'Junior Gymnast of the Year' competition in 1982. She was Athletics captain in her final year at NULS, 1988, and subsequently gained a PhD in Acousto-optics from Sheffield University before joining a circus as an acrobat. She performed (right) in a series of idents aired by the BBC between programmes. Her earliest training was at Old Girl Minnie Skerrett's School of Dance.

Following a visit to Orme House, the Archbishop of Canterbury's wife, Mrs Runcie, invited Orme House pupils to help plant trees at Lambeth Palace. Subsequent invitations were issued to barbecues in the grounds and to help clear leaves. An account of the 1989 trip forms part of an OH 'diary' in which pupils recorded their view of events during the year.

Above: Graham Stanley (Stan, the ice cream man) retired in May 1990. Bill Donaldson presented a salver to mark the occasion, although Stan was not always so popular. Stan's ice cream van was banned in 1959, leading to articles in the *Sentinel* and a gaudy 'Ice cream sold here' banner being swung from the school flagpole. Michael James – former pupil and staff member – can be seen behind the salver.

Right: Dr Ray Reynolds became the schools' second principal in 1990 and retired in 2002. A graduate of Queen's University, Belfast with a PhD in Physics, Ray moved to NULS from Millfield School, Somerset. Academic standards remained high during Ray's tenure – 163 students gained Oxbridge places over the period.

Opposite above: In 1966, Mr and Mrs Pugh donated the greenhouse on the left of this 1993 aerial view. An extension alongside the Memorial Hall, the David Cohen Suite, was added in 2004. This supports activities in the Memorial Hall itself or in the extension. David was Chairman of Governors for twenty-five years, playing a key role in the successful establishment of NULS in the independent sector.

Left: To mark the centenary of the formation of the Old Girls' Society (OGS), a china figurine of an Orme Girl, complete with hockey stick, hat, red bag and girdle was commissioned. To assist the maker, Francesca China, pupil Gemma Baggaley acted as a model. Old Girls bought 450 of the figurines.

Below: In 1992, a party of forty-two pupils, teachers, friends and parents visited China.

The 1936-built Orme Girls' 'temporary' annexe was finally demolished in 1994. Many pupils enjoyed the unusual features of this wooden building, such as the domed floor! Initially replaced by another temporary wooden structure containing two classrooms, the purpose-built Millennium Sixth Form Centre now occupies the site. This was formally opened by the Lord Lieutenant of Staffordshire, Mr James Hawley, in September 2000. Built at a cost of around £800,000, the Sixth Form Centre provided three new teaching rooms, an ICT suite, toilet facilities and a large Sixth Form Common Room.

In 1995, Kerry Buckingham and Sarah Turner received Certificates of Excellence from the Oxford and Cambridge Schools' Examination Board 'in recognition of outstanding performance' at A-Level. The Board awards a maximum of three certificates in any syllabus. Kerry was among five NULS students who gained places at Cambridge that year, and Sarah one of ten at Oxford.

Tim Barlow played for England Under-18s against Wales and France in 1995, becoming the first pupil in the school's history to be awarded an International rugby cap. On behalf of the school, Ray Reynolds accepted Tim's donation of his shirt.

Above: Paul Jerrum, Head of Orme House from 1994 to 2004, entertains the pupils at the 1998 Christmas party.

Right: Science teachers Simon Williams and Mark Snell organised a Science Fair in 1997 which over 3,500 visitors attended. The special guest was Michaela Strachan from the BBC's *Really Wild Show.* The purpose of the fair was to promote an understanding and an enthusiasm for science amongst younger children, specifically eight-to-fourteen year olds. There were over fifty exhibits enabling visitors to both see and experience science in action.

A number of reunions are run by the Castilians at the school each year. The 1997 Five-Year Reunion for those who left five years earlier, in 1992, was held in the Victoria Library. From left to right: Chris Farmer, Claire Bloor, Rob Irving, Margaret Atkins.

Dr Ray Reynolds and OH pupils in the new garden alongside the gymnasium, with the Victoria Library in the background. Ray officially opened the Charlotte Pitt-designed garden, funded by the OH Parents Association, in December 1999.

To raise funds for the Donna Louise Trust, OH pupils paid £1 for the privilege of wearing denim in March 2000. Status Quo drummer Jeff Rich visited the school on the day and set his drum kit up in the Memorial Hall. As well as playing the drums himself, Jeff spoke on the history of drums and gave some pupils a chance to try playing different types of drum.

During the 2000 summer holiday, David Light added murals to the exterior of two of the gymnasium walls on the Victoria Road site. These depict the various seasons of the year and remain a distinctive feature. The OH Parents Association largely met the cost.

An all-weather floodlit pitch was opened in 2002 by former England and Great Britain Women's Hockey captain Jane Sixsmith OBE. This greatly enhanced the options available for sports and is heavily used. During construction of the AstroTurf on the Lower Close, old wartime trenches filled with pottery waste and old drainage pipes were discovered.

Ray Reynolds retired as principal in Summer 2002 and was succeeded by Rob Dillow. Cambridge graduate Rob was a civil servant at the Foreign Office before moving into education as a languages specialist. As part of the fundraising effort for her participation in the World Challenge Expedition to Namibia in Summer 2003, pupil Paula Hannant produced a calendar featuring staff members. Rob Dillow is in the centre, complete with mortarboard.

After interviewing Major Albert Mitchell (centre), the president of the Newcastle Normandy Veterans Association, Helen Boldon (left) took first place in the 2003 national Spirit of Normandy Trust Contest with her article, 'Reflections on Normandy 1944'. Danielle Linsell (right) and Emma Tonks (second right) helped with research for the article.

Angela Hartill, who succeeded Paul Jerrum as Head of Orme House in 2004, with Pre-preparatory and Nursery Department staff in the £2 million purpose-built building, opened in September 2004.

Other local titles published by Tempus

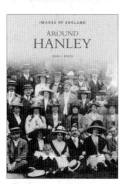

Newcastle-under-Lyme Revisited

NEIL COLLINGWOOD AND GREGOR SHUFFLEBOTHAM

This fascinating collection of over 200 archive images, many previously unpublished, explores the historic market town of Newcastle-under-Lyme, from Victorian times to the present day. Detailed captions accompany each picture, bringing the images to life and providing vivid accounts of events in Newcastle over the last 150 years. The buildings, shops and industries of the town are described, as well as transport, local schools, the services and of course local people, always at the heart of this strong community.

0 7524 3672 4

Around Hanley

JOHN S. BOOTH

This fascinating collection of photographs illustrates life as it was in and around the pottery town of Hanley. Originally just a single farm, Hanley grew into the largest and most central town in the greater area of Stoke-on-Trent, blossoming in the early twentieth century with the development of heavy industry. This pictorial history reflects the town as it was at that time, at the height of its success.

0 7524 3407 1

Biddulph Volume II

DEREK J. WHEELHOUSE

This second absorbing collection of over 200 images traces some of the changes and developments in Biddulph over the last century. Drawn from the archives of the Biddulph & District Historical and Genealogical Society, this valuable pictorial history highlights some of the events that have taken place during this time as well as exploring aspects of everyday life, from schools and shops to transport and modern restoration programmes.

0 7524 3463 2

Burslem

THE BURSLEM HISTORY CLUB

Using over 200 evocative images, this book documents the people and places of Burslem, the Mother Town of the Potteries. The Burslem Angel and the Old Fire Station are featured, as well as many of the grand Victorian buildings and the factories, schools and churches of the area. Many significant events are also recorded, including the Sneyd Pit disaster of 1942.

0 7524 3456 X

If you are interested in purchasing other books published by Tempus, or in case you have difficulty finding any Tempus books in your local bookshop, you can also place orders directly through our website

www.tempus-publishing.com